FRANCISCO CALVO SERRALLER

Masterpieces

Fundación Amigos del Museo
del Prado

Floor plan of the Prado Museum

SECOND FLOOR

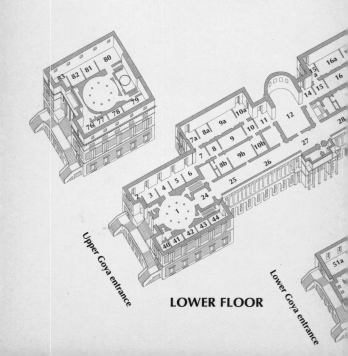

LOWER FLOOR

Upper Goya entrance

Lower Goya entrance

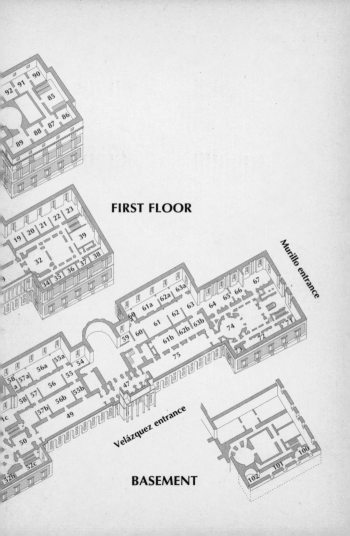

FIRST FLOOR

Murillo entrance

Velázquez entrance

BASEMENT

First Edition: March 2003

Cover and interior design: Ángel Uriarte
Axonometric projections: Ana Pazó Espinosa
Translation: Everett Rice
Edition: Carmen Ponce de León and Manuel Florentín

© Francisco Calvo Serraller, 2002
© Fundación Amigos del Museo del Prado
   ISBN: 84-95452-12-X
   Depósito legal: M-14.910-2003
   Printed in Closas-Orcoyen, S. L. Paracuellos del Jarama (Madrid)
   Printed in Spain

Introduction

The Prado Museum was inaugurated on 19 November 1819, making it one of the oldest public art museums in the world. The Museum emerged from the initiative of King Ferdinand VII, who donated a substantial part of the very rich collections of the monarchs of Spain. For this reason the institution was originally called the Royal Museum of Painting and Sculpture.

This not only explains the origins of its collections, but also the identity of its owner, governing authority, and protector. In reality, until 1865, when the Museum was entailed as crown property in an implicit form of nationalization, the destiny of this prestigious institution was uncertain, depending as it did upon the volition and the fate of the occupants of the Spanish throne.

From the beginning the Prado Museum has been located in what is still its principal building, and its only building for a long time. It was designed by one of the best Spanish architects of the eighteenth century, Juan de Villanueva, and was initially conceived to comply with an official commission to build a Royal Museum of Natural Sciences. Work began in 1785 and was practically finished by 1808 at the outbreak of the Peninsular War in which the Spaniards were faced with Napoleon's invasion.

The architect Villanueva was already dead when the museum´s destiny finally became clear and his student, Antonio López Aguado was chosen to carry out the task of restoration, adaptation, and completion. Since that time this historic edifice has been submitted to several projects of enlargement and improvement, as well as for providing new technical and operational services related to an ever-increasing number of visitors and new criteria of museology.

The most recent phase of expansion and improvement of services is slated for completion in the year 2004. Aside from the work that has already been completed or is still in progress in the main building, the Prado Museum has spread to other buildings such as the so-called *Casón del Buen Retiro*, which for years has housed the Museum´s collection of nineteenth-century Spanish art and which, at present, is also undergoing a process of remodelling.

The name of the Casón del Buen Retiro comes from having been the ballroom of the Buen Retiro Palace, built in the seventeenth century by Philip IV and now partially destroyed. Another part of this palace which was originally the Hall of Realms has, until recently, been the home of the Spanish Army Museum whose collection is now being moved elsewhere. This part of the historic palace has been assigned to the Prado Museum and its function will be decided upon in the next few years.

As for the collection of the Prado Museum, it is worth remembering that when the Museum was opened it housed a selection of 331 works of the Spanish School up to Goya, who at the time was still alive. From that first moment onwards, the collection has grown and become more diversified, so that it is now composed of nearly ten thousand works. From a quantitative point of view, the Prado Museum´s current collection no longer derives in its greater part from the original bequests of the sovereigns of Spain but their legacy has left an indelible stamp on the aesthetic definition of the whole.

Unlike other museums of similar importance, the collection of the Prado Museum is not complete and balanced, but in purely pictorial terms it is perhaps the most singular and intense. The Prado Museum is logically the most significant collection of Spanish art of the past, but it has incomparable representations of other national schools such as the Venetians, the Neapolitans, or the Flemish, apart from gaps in other schools or periods. The legal and administrative organization of the Prado Museum has undergone many changes during its long history, which will soon reach its second centenary.

Whatever the Museum's history has been, the present situation fits the description of a national public museum which is state-owned and regulated by law as an "autonomous institution" managed by a Director-General and a Royal Board of Trustees composed of twenty members, among whom there are officials from various government institutions, former directors of the Museum, recognized specialists and other distinguished representatives of cultural sectors such as private collectors.

The internal organization of the Museum is divided into three principal areas of responsibility: Conservation, Management, and Development and

External Relations which, in turn, are subdivided into various departments. The present staff, including gallery attendants and other technical services, number three hundred and ninety-two. Finally, mention must also be made of the support given to the Museum, since 1980, by the Friends of the Prado Museum Foundation whose current president is the Duke of Soria.

LOWER FLOOR

1. **Fra Angelico:** The Annunciation Altarpiece. Room 49.
2. **Mantegna:** The Dormition of the Virgin Mary. Room 49.
3. **Raphael:** Portrait of a Cardinal. Room 49.
4. **Van der Weyden:** The Descent from the Cross. Room 58.
5. **Bosch:** The Garden of Earthly Delights. Room 56a.
6. **Patenier:** Charon Crossing the River Styx. Room 56a.
7. **Dürer:** Adam and Eve. Room 54.
8. **Titian:** Charles V at the Battle of Mühlberg. Room 61.
9. **Tintoretto:** Christ Washing the Feet of the Apostles. Room 75.
10. **Veronese:** Venus and Adonis. Room 62b.
11. **El Greco:** Gentleman with Hand on Chest. Room 60a.

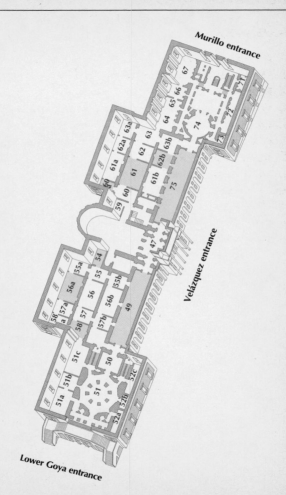

Murillo entrance

Velázquez entrance

Lower Goya entrance

51a 51b 51c 50 52a 52b 52c 51 58 57a 58a 56a 55a 54 57 56 55 53b 57b 49 56b 55b 59 60 61 62a 63a 50 61a 62 63 64 65 66 67 61b 62b 63b 74 72 75 73 73a 47

11

Fra Angelico: *The Annunciation Altarpiece*
(Cat. No. 15)

This altarpiece was painted around 1426-1427 for the church of the Convent of San Domenico in Fiesole where the artist Guido di Pietro took vows as a Dominican friar under the name of Fra Giovanni da Fiesole, although he was later to be known as Fra Angelico. For many years this work was held in doubt as to its attribution, but today it is considered to be one of the best and most "revolutionary" works created by the singular friar-painter whose personal virtues and pious subjects have sometimes overshadowed the recognition of his talent. This altarpiece consists of a panel in which the scene of the Annunciation is preceded by the Expulsion of Adam and Eve from the Garden of Eden, since the subject is essentially redemption from original sin, and a predella with five smaller panels which represent episodes of the life of the Virgin Mary: the Birth and Betrothal of the Virgin; the Visitation; the Adoration of the Magi; the Presentation of Jesus in the Temple; and the Dormition of the Virgin. Fra Angelico conceived all of these Marian scenes according to the latest criteria of perspective and he substituted Nature for the conventional gold background, as demanded by the generation of Brunelleschi, Donatello, and Masaccio. Fra Angelico was born in 1400 and died in 1455. When he began his artistic career, before his profession as a Dominican, the so-called International Gothic style was predominant. He himself must have trained as a miniaturist and illuminator although he later adopted the new ideas of the Renaissance. His sincere and intense piety, which he expressed in painting with exquisite refinement and deep emotion,

has often distracted his admirers from the novelty of his approach to form. But he has now been confirmed as one of the protagonists of artistic change and the most important Florentine master after 1430. This altarpiece was acqui-

red in the seventeenth century by the Duke of Lerma, who installed it in the church of the Dominicans in Valladolid. It was later taken to the Descalzas Reales Monastery in Madrid and moved to the Prado Museum in 1861.

Andrea Mantegna: *The Dormition of the Virgin Mary*
(Cat. No. 248)

The Spanish writer and art critic Eugenio d´Ors attracted our attention to this work in his book *Three Hours in the Prado Museum* (1922) when he affirmed that this was his favourite painting. This is a small panel painting in tempera, 54 x 42 cm, dated around 1461 and a fragment of a larger work that was cut down. Except for the fragment in the Prado only the upper part, representing *Christ with the Soul of the Virgin Mary*, survives in a collection in Ferrara.

This has led scholars to believe that the complete work originally formed part of the decoration of the chapel that Ludovico Gonzaga commissioned Mantegna to paint in 1459. Andrea Mantegna was born in 1431 and died in 1506. He was educated in Padua and early on displayed all the qualities of the Renaissance style that is characteristic of northern Italy: clarity of line, a sophisticated knowledge of antiquity, and a surprising command of perspective and foreshortening. In the Prado panel we find these qualities in the their greatest splendour: in the accuracy of the background with its fine landscape, skilfully framed by a window through which we can recognize the lake of Mantua and the bridge of San Giorgio, and in the foreground, an imaginary chamber with flanking pilasters and a chequered marble floor.

The Virgin Mary has "fallen asleep" in the presence of the Apostles whose individualized features are especially precise. The solemn dignity and spirituality that reigns over the scene is intensified by the attitudes and the solidity of the figures, who seem to be grouped in a geometric order in which each

form and each line has its symmetrical equivalent. The real and the unreal are united in a manner that is seldom attained in art, even at the height of the fifteenth century. Mantegna was highly regarded in his own time and he influenced Giovanni Bellini and Albrecht Dürer but, rarity of rarities, his prestige has remained intact up to the present day.

Raphael: *Portrait of a Cardinal*
(Cat. No. 299)

After years of debate, this portrait of an unidentified cardinal is now unquestionably considered to be the best of the Prado Museum's far from insignificant collection of works by Raffaello Sanzio, known in English as Raphael, who was born in 1483 and died in 1520. Specialists are inclined to date this portrait towards 1510, two years after the artist settled in Rome at the invitation of Pope Julius II. If indeed it is the best, we find ourselves not only before a work that dates from the beginning of the golden maturity of this artist, who died at the age of thirty-seven, but also one that belongs to the gloriously decisive moment called the "moment of classicism" in the Renaissance when the protagonists were Leonardo da Vinci, Michelangelo, and Raphael himself. This composition (oil on panel) shows a seated half-length figure, turned slightly into a three-quarter view against a dark background. The red of the cardinal's vestments stands out against this dark background with sumptuous brilliance in the slippery folds of the watered silk. The sober and effective chromatic contrasts are interrupted only by the white of the cardinal's sleeve. Raphael has used a tenuous light to illuminate the young face with its inquisitive strabismic gaze, its tight thin lips, refined features and distant, enigmatic expression. It is obvious that we are in the

presence of a complex personality whose fearful meanders are revealed with supreme mastery in this portrait. This mastery Raphael had acquired not only in what he had learned from Perugino but also from Flemish models and the subtle shading of Leonardo. With Raphael the art of portraiture attained a perfect balance between the real and the unreal which, as in the present case, raises the individua-lity of a specific person to the level of a prototype. The researcher Luisa Becherruci believes that this cardinal was Francesco Alidosi, a papal legate reputed to be a cold intriguer, who was assassinated in 1510 at the hands of Francesco Maria della Rovere.

Rogier van der Weyden: *The Descent from the Cross*
(Cat. No. 2825)

Probably painted around 1432-1435, this is one of Van der Weyden's most famous and highly regarded works. Van der Weyden (1399/1400-1464) was among the finest Flemish painters of the mid-fifteenth century. Much as been said as to whether this painting was the central panel of a triptych the wings of which have been lost. It was commissioned by the Crossbowmen's Guild for the Church of Our Lady Outside the Walls in Louvain. In the sixteenth century it was acquired by Queen Mary of Hungary and later entered the collection of Philip II at the Monastery of El Escorial. It was moved to the Prado Museum in 1939. As with much of the little-known early work of Van der Weyden, the question has arisen as to whether this *Descent from the Cross* might have been painted by Robert Campin, also known as the Master of Flémalle, but the work has a new dramatic vigour that refutes such hypotheses. The modelling of the figures that stand out from a plain gold back wall is so strong that we are made to think of sculpture, above all in the bold relief

produced by the shadows that surround them and the impressive treatment of the drapery the folds of which are contoured with a firmness that seems to have been accomplished with a chisel. But neither the strongly defined relief, the roundedness of the forms and volumes nor the individualized treatment given to each one of the large figures diminishes the atmosphere of intense drama that pervades the whole work. And neither of these traits overwhelms the precision of the most insignificant details. The composition is complex and sophisticated, because it wraps the figures in a sort of ellipse where each personality is paired off according to a well-calculated order of equivalents, for example in the inclined central figures of the dead Christ and the swooning Virgin

Mary. This work raises the expression of emotion to levels hitherto unknown, but it never falls into simple striving for effect. The realism of the faces has become a milestone in the art of portraiture.

Hieronymus Bosch: *The Garden of Earthly Delights* (Cat. No. 2823)

Hieronymus van Aeken took the name Bosch from s' Hertogenbosch, the town in North Brabant where he was born around 1450 and where he died in 1516. From what we know, Bosch led the life of a well-to-do man. The full extent of his artistic production is unknown, and the forty probable works that have survived are undated, making it difficult to establish a chronological sequence. Bosch was a fervent Catholic and his subjects are conventional, but they are interspersed with symbols that are extremely complicated and fantastic. This makes his work fascinating but it also puts the imagination of his interpreters to the test. Their multiple speculations have not always been well founded. The Prado Museum owns several of Bosch's best and most famous paintings, thanks to the Philip II's enthusiasm for his work. Philip II apparently held Bosch's moralizing fantasies and his misanthropy in high esteem, even when the artist's style had gone out of fashion. Bosch was greatly admired by his contemporaries but his real apotheosis has occurred in our own time, as psychologists and surrealists have come to see his work as an incomparable milestone of originality and inventiveness. The triptych of *The Garden of Earthly Delights* (oil on panel) is undoubtedly one of Bosch's most important works. When the outer wings of the triptych are closed we see the third day of the Creation of the World.

When they are open, from left to right we find the Garden of Eden and Adam and Eve, at whose feet swarm some of the bizarre creatures that symbolize the offen- ces and the sins of mankind. The right-hand panel represents the lugubrious precincts of Hell in which the damned souls are being submitted to all sorts of tor-

ments. In the central panel we observe the radiant and tumultuous ebullience of several nude figures who, in total abandon, are engaging in all manner of carnal pleasures. It is precisely in this central panel where Bosch's fantasy reaches its greatest height. It is here that we find his most extraordinary inventiveness, the most surprising alterations of size and proportion, the most exotic creatures and environments, and the most sophisticated and extravagant symbols, in a dream world that is unsurpassable. Bosch was a learned man of great culture. The awesome wealth of visual metaphors that he invented stems from a very rich tradition and a vision of life that are never simple. Consequently, the torrent of interpretive hypotheses which his work has prompted has never really managed to unlock the mysterious depths of this great painter's mind.

Joachim Patenier: *Charon Crossing the River Styx*
(Cat. No. 1616)

Patenier is a rather curious artist about whom we know very little. Only a few of his works have survived and not many of them are signed. He was born at Dinant around 1485 and died in Antwerp in 1524. He settled in Antwerp around 1515. Albrecht Dürer met Patenier during a trip to the Low Countries and he made a drawing of him. One of the sources of information we have about Patenier is what Dürer wrote about him in his journal. He described Patenier as a "good landscape painter" and this is confirmed in Patenier´s known works. In fact, Patenier is considered to be a pioneer of landscape painting as an independent genre. He had no problem about letting a landscape background become the dominant element of his pictures. His main figures are often dwarfed by their natural surroundings, as for example in *Charon Crossing the River Styx*, an oil painting on panel which is probably Patenier's best landscape. All of Patenier's best qualities are present here: an extraordinary sense of naturalistic observation and representation of details along with an almost fantastic atmosphere that lends the whole painting an entrancingly mysterious air. The composition is centred

on Charon, the Greek mythological boatman, who is ferrying a dead soul to Hades. The source of the subject matter is, most surely, Dante's epic account since several details of Patenier's painting coincide with the written narrative. Except for the gigantic figure of Charon, all of the other details seem lost in in the wide sweeping vista of an otherworldly landscape. But if the viewer looks carefully he will discover the mouth of Hell on the right and on the left, the beauty of Elysium, the pagan version of Paradise. The cardinal elements of this composition are its vibrant dark-green luminosity streaked with radiant emerald, the distant horizon with its equally radiant sky, the precision of the details of every part of Nature represented, and finally, the enveloping mystery of the whole atmosphere. The surrealistic appearance of this picture leads us to think of Patenier as the link between Bosch and Brueghel.

Albrecht Dürer: *Adam and Eve*
(Cat. No. 2177 and 2178)

This diptych in oil on panel was painted by Dürer after his second trip to Venice, when he returned to his native Nuremberg at the beginning of his splendid maturity. Adam and Eve are marvellous ideal representations of the male and female nude, a theme that obsessed the artist and became the subject of his celebrated and highly influential treatise on the proportions of the human body which was published posthumously in 1528, the year of his death at the age of fifty-seven. These two studies of the nude were painted in 1507, three years after the artist had made an engraving of the same subject. The artistic progress that Dürer had made in those three years can be appreciated in the Prado nudes where he seems much less dependent upon antiquity or symbolic data. Here he concentrates solely on the ideal proportions of the human figure, clearly conceived on the basis of Classical models but without any need for specific supporting elements. He has eliminated the landscape that appeared in the background of the earlier engraving as well as any other details that might distract our attention from the beauty of these two young bodies whose precise contours, sharply Germanic in origin, or whose realist features and other details do not diminish a certain sensuality or a firm and penetrating expressiveness. The importance of this work for the artist himself is confirmed by the fact that they were not painted on commission. He painted them for his own use, most surely in response to his striving for the canon of ideal beauty that had always engaged his interest. But the aforementioned second journey to Italy must have provided an even greater

stimulus when he came into contact with the ideas on this matter among the followers of Leonardo da Vinci. In the present work Dürer seems to have achie- ved a perfect balance bet- ween Germanic artistic tra- dition and the models of the Italian Renaissance. In this sense *Adam and Eve* is a milestone not only in

Dürer's own career but also in the study of the nude as a genre in modern Western painting.

Titian: *Charles V at the Battle of Mühlberg* (Cat. No. 410)

Tiziano Vecellio, know in English as Titian, was born in 1485 and died in 1576 at the age of ninety-one. He was undoubtedly the greatest painter of the Venetian School, which had such a decisive influence on Spanish art. Titian is well represented in the Prado Museum and not surprisingly so since the relationship between Charles V and his son Philip II went beyond the limits of mere commissions and became almost an obsession for both monarchs, as reflected in the ample correspondence that has survived. This explains the abundance, variety, and quality of Titian´s work in the Prado, as well as the fact that the artist seems almost to have been the official portraitist to these two powerful monarchs and practically to have invented their complex imagery of royal power. One of the most remarkable of these works is the equestrian portrait of Charles V which Titian was commissioned to paint in 1548, to commemorate Charles´s victory over the Protestant troops of the Schmalkaldic League at the Battle of Mühlberg, on the banks of the Elbe River. Titian painted this portrait during his second stay in Augsburg, which explains the astonishing fidelity of the likeness of Charles V and the surroundings of the famous battle, where the artist faithfully reproduces the real landscape. The armoured monarch and his mount, advancing in solitude, lance at the ready, over a beau-

tiful landscape at dusk form an image of prodigious accuracy in the bearing, the clothing, and the composure of the sovereign as recounted by the chronicles of this glorious event. In addition to his colourful realism Titian has captured a complex range of symbolic allusions. On the one hand, the model for this image was the equestrian statue of Marcus Aurelius, but there are also deeper undertones in several details such as the lance, which refers to the spear of Longinus at the Crucifixion; the reddish setting sun, to the sun that stood still for Joshua; and the Elbe River in the background, to the Rubicon of Roman history. Elements from the classical, medieval, and modern worlds are superimposed, converting the figure of the victorious monarch into a prototype of the Classical-Christian ideal. Titian´s virtuosity in the equation of colour and light make this portrait a masterpiece in which several elements coexist. In spite of the many extraordinary works by Titian that accompany it in the Prado Museum, this portrait is exceptional.

Tintoretto: *Christ Washing the Feet of the Apostles*
(Cat. No. 2824)

Painted in 1547, this enormous horizontal canvas (210 x 533 cm) was originally placed in the presbytery of the Church of San Marcuola in Venice. It depicts the well-known scene from Saint John's Gospel in which Christ washed the feet of his disciples before the Last Supper. Tintoretto has interpreted the subject freely, above all with regard to the setting he has invented, which not only converts the room into a large, sumptuous chamber in a palace, but through the openings of the loggia we also see a row of buildings that are clearly reminiscent of Venice. Jacopo Robusti, called "Il Tintoretto" because his father was a dyer, lived from 1518 to 1594. His production was immense, his works are

filled with passion, and his technical virtuosity is spectacular, in spite of the impediments he encountered in the rivalry of his colleagues and because of his own complex and difficult temperament. He was endowed with a prodigious sense of objective detail which is sometimes filled with intense emotion, but his genius truly shines in the monumental compositions where his lively two-point perspective produces an effect of vertigo. He shows his inimitable mastery of foreshortening in the way he places his figures in highly forced postures against distant horizons. All of these splendid qualities can be found in the present canvas in which the viewer is drawn in not only by the lively interplay of perspectival relationships but also by the subtle gradations of light and shadow that produce an atmosphere which joins the picture space to the real space of the viewer. The figures of Christ and His disciples are treated with naturalism but the architecture that surrounds them is so imaginatively idealized that it seems more like the delirium of a dream.

Veronese: *Venus and Adonis*
(Cat. No. 482)

Paolo Caliari changed his name to Veronese, after Verona, the city where he was born around 1528. Towards 1553 he settled in Venice, where he painted the better part of his known work until his death in 1588. Veronese is rightly considered to be one of the most illustrious masters of Venetian painting in the sixteenth century. Along with his rival Tintoretto he was the most splendid of the artists who came after Titian. This period of Venetian painting is undoubtedly the best represented in the Prado Museum. This also explains the quality of the works by Veronese in the Museum's collection. One of the most remarkable is this *Venus and Adonis*, which is also important for having been acquired in Venice by Velázquez, perhaps around 1650, during his second journey to Italy where he was entrusted with enriching the art collection of Philip IV. Velázquez purchased both this *Venus and Adonis* and its companion *Cephalus and Procris* since the two paintings develop an elegiac reflection on the dangers of the hunt. The story of the love of Venus and Adonis is taken from Ovid's *Metamorphoses* and the artist has chosen the moment in which the goddess keeps an uneasy watch over her lover's slumber, as if she could already foresee the fate of Adonis when he took up his passion for the hunt again. Veronese dearly loved ostentation, grand settings, the sensuality of the nude, and the dazzling beauty of sumptuous cloth such as brocade. The artist applied all of his best qualities in this composition, which dates from the decade of the 1560's. These qualities are resplendent not only in the brilliant and original colour and in the masterly high-

lights that emphasize them, but also in the well-calculated drama of the atmosphere in which he presents the crux of the story that tilts between unreserved abandon and an anxious presentiment of death. Unlike Tintoretto, Veronese transmits these emotions in a subtle and serene manner, without spasmodic agitation or atmospheric turbulence.

El Greco: *Gentleman with Hand on Chest*
(Cat. No. 809)

Signed in Greek capital letters but undated, this portrait is generally considered to have been painted around 1580, a few years after Domenikos Theotokopoulos, called El Greco, arrived in Spain. El Greco was born in Candia, the capital of the island of Crete, in 1541 and after consecutive sojourns in Venice and Rome which helped him to "westernize" and modernize his style, he settled in Toledo where he lived and worked until his death in 1614. El Greco not only reached his artistic maturity in Spain, he would also exercise a decisive influence on Spanish taste which would bear fruit in the seventeenth century. He was initially greeted with distrust in Spain, especially in the circles of the court of Philip II. But neither his Mannerist style, his foreignness, nor his rather extravagant sophistication kept his contemporaries from praising his outstanding talent as a portraitist, not even when the exaggerations of his later period frightened practically everybody. A clear and popular example of the general esteem for El Greco as a portrait painter is precisely this image of an unknown *Gentleman with Hand on Chest* which has traditionally been considered a physical and moral prototype of the Spanish *hidalgo*. The attitude of placing his hand on his chest has been interpreted as a gesture of protocol upon taking an oath of office. This has lead some scholars to affirm that the gentleman might be Juan de Silva Ribera, knight of the Order of Santiago, Marquess of Montemayor, and chief notary of Toledo. The recent restoration of this painting has revealed, even more clearly than before, the deformation of the gentleman's left shoulder, and

33

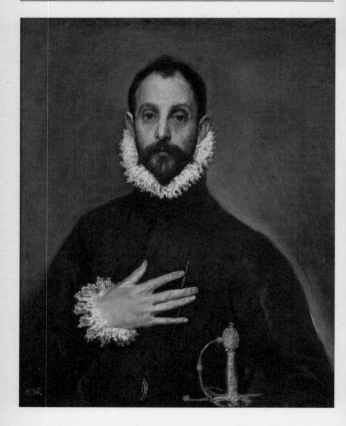

this has caused other scholars to think of Juan de Silva Silveira, knight of the Order of Calatrava and Count of Portalegre, who was left incapacitated by a harquebus-shot wound in the Battle of Alcázarquivir in 1598. In any case, this half-length portrait has a rigidity and frontality that gives the sitter a solemn and hieratic appearance, which is accentuated by the black costume and the velvety grey background. El Greco's skilful treatment of the slender hilt of the sword, the light that falls on the face and the hand, and the pensive expression on the face, all lend the sitter an air of distant elegance and austerity that would later be considered very Spanish.

FIRST FLOOR

12. **Poussin:** Apollo and the Muses on Mount Parnassus. Room 3.
13. **Claude Lorrain:** The Embarkation of Saint Paula at Ostia. Room 2.
14. **Rembrandt:** Artemisia. Room 7.
15. **Rubens:** The Three Graces. Room 9.
16. **Ribera:** Jacob´s Dream. Room 26.
17. **Velázquez:** Las Meninas. Room 12.
18. **Zurbarán:** Agnus Dei. Room 18.
19. **Murillo:** The Patrician´s Dream. Room 29.
20. **Goya:** The Family of Charles IV. Room 32.

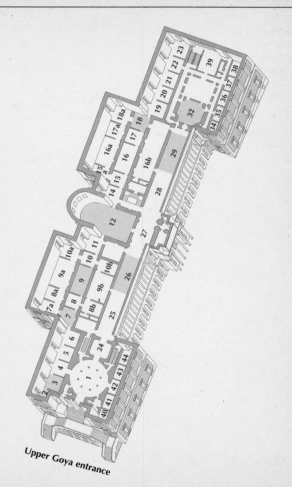

Upper Goya entrance

Nicolas Poussin: *Apollo and the Muses on Mount Parnassus* (Cat. No. 2313)

Together with the *The Triumph of David*, this *Apollo and the Muses* is the most beautiful painting by Poussin in the Prado Museum. Each one of these paintings has its own atmosphere, due to the different subjects represented. The former is filled with melancholy, even though it celebrates a victory; the latter has an aura of calm plenitude, as befits the subject of Parnassus. What we see here is the god Apollo surrounded by the nine Muses and at his feet, a nude nymph, reclining next to a spring that flows from Mount Helion (Parnassus). In the foreground, on either side of the central group, there are several male figures whose laurel crowns indicate that they are poets. The question of the identity of these poets has produced more debate than convincing hypotheses. In any case, it is clear that we are contemplating a painting that uses the appropriate mythological setting to celebrate poetic inspiration. Poussin's own source of inspiration for this composition was most certainly the Parnassus that Raphael painted for the Stanza della Segnatura in the papal apartments of the Vatican. Poussin's homage to Raphael, the painter that fascinated him most during his first years in Rome, beginning in 1524, is not the work of a servile follower but rather the homage of a very personal and free admirer. This work was painted around 1631-1632 when Poussin, who was born in 1593/4 not only was about to celebrate his fortieth birthday but also after he had overcome a serious illness and had just married. In this painting we can recognize all the characteristics of Poussin's maturity as an artist who, despite the lingering influence of Titian, was by

that time entirely focused on Classicism.

Particularly notable is the simple and clear articulation of vertical and horizontal lines, as well as the beautiful chromatic scale of blues and golds. An atmosphere of serene and radiant joy permeates the entire picture, which reflects a pure ideal. There is nothing sombre nor anything that denotes a certain moral reserve in this painting. It is the triumph of all that is limpid and transparent.

Claude Lorrain: *The Embarkation of Saint Paula at Ostia*
(Cat. No. 2254)

Painted in 1639, this vertical canvas is one of four paintings of the same format in the second commission that Claude Lorrain received from Philip IV for the decoration of the Buen Retiro Palace in Madrid. This commission was a great boost to the career of Claude Gellée, called Claude in English, who was born in 1600 in what was at that time the independent duchy of Lorraine. As a youth Claude went to Rome where he worked as a pastry-cook in the house of the painter Agostino Tassi. This changed his destiny because, unlike painters with conventional training, Claude was to specialize in landscape, a genre that was beginning to emerge but hitherto had not been held in very high artistic esteem. Claude later earned fame and fortune enough not only to receive important commissions but also to have to protect himself from many contemporary forgers by means of a catalogue of drawings he made after his finished works. Claude brought a poetic sensibility to the Classical ideal of landscape which was formulated in the seventeenth century. Using a raking light he created a lyrically dramatic and almost proto-Romantic atmosphere that envelopes the small figures that move about in the spectacular natural settings of his works. The present painting represents the story of Saint Paula, a Roman matron who, after she was left a widow, set out for the Holy Land in the year 385, to follow Saint Jerome. Claude has depicted the embarkation in the Roman port of Ostia, where we see Saint Paula in the difficult moment of separating from her only son, and setting out with her daughters Paulina, Eustochium, and Rufina on a journey of

pious but uncertain destination. Apart from what we can make out of these figures and the others that are distributed throughout the scene, Claude's composition is centred on the powerful flood of light that comes from the rising sun and engulfs the whole architectural setting of Renaissance buildings that are graded almost at a right angle to the picture plane, thus creating a corridor for the beam of light. This masterpiece comes from Claude's early period and prefigures the port scenes of his maturity.

Rembrandt: *Artemisia (also called "Sophonisba")* (Cat. No. 2132)

The origins of the Prado Museum's collection in the legacy of the monarchs of Spain reflects not only their personal tastes but the political history of the country as well. The Museum has only a few lesser works by the Dutch painters of the seventeenth century, but there are notable exceptions such as this painting by Rembrandt. It is the Prado's only, albeit marvellous example of this artist´s work. The canvas is signed and dated 1634, the year in which Rembrandt married Saskia van Uylenburgh, perhaps the happiest period of the artist's life. Rembrandt was already in complete command of his characteristically brilliant technique with its golden light. Here we find Rembrandt with all of his exceptional talents in their fullness: naturalism, psychological insight, perfect dramatic atmosphere, and dazzling virtuosity in the treatment of details, above all in the objects, the costumes, and in the textures of fabrics. Doubts as to the identity of the historical personage represented by this resplendent young matron come from the fact

that it could either be So-
phonisba, daughter of the
Carthaginian general Has-
drubal and wife of King
Masinissa who, when she
was taken prisoner by the
Roman general Scipio,
drank the poison sent to
her by her husband in
order to avoid any possi-
ble dishonour; or it could
be Artemisia, the widow of
the Persian ruler Mauso-
leus, to whom she erected
a magnificent funerary
monument at Halicarnas-
sus, the *Mausoleum*, and
who tried to become a
living tomb for her husband
by drinking his ashes mixed
with water or wine. In any
case, both stories exalt
amorous fidelity beyond
the grave. Even though the
subject and the year in
which the picture was exe-

cuted lead us to identify the features of the painted figure with those of Saskia, the artist's wife, it is possible that Rembrandt did not have a specific model in mind because he was creating a prototype. This does not mean that the artist did not take pains in the representation of the dress of this splendid figure or that of the servant who is offering her the drink in its exotic cup. Neither did Rembrandt fail subtly to capture the facial expression of this stately woman, who seems lost in thought, or the flashes of golden light that fall on her face and become even more luminous as they are bathed in deep shadows.

Peter Paul Rubens: *The Three Graces*
(Cat. No. 1670)

The Three Graces was probably painted between 1636 and 1638, towards the end of Rubens' career and very full life. It is among the best of his paintings in the Prado Museum, which houses one of the most complete collection of works by this brilliant Flemish painter. Rubens was born by coincidence in Siegen, Westphalia in 1577 and died in Antwerp in 1640. *The Three Graces* is a compendium of all of Rubens' virtues: a Classical theme developed with the discernment of an erudite man who was also a great expert on art; the female nude, in which Rubens´ sensuality and refinement reached their moment of greatest expressiveness; the exquisite painterly manner that he attained in his later years when he was in the fullness of his powers as an artist, his fame, and his personal happiness, and when his art had become a grateful celebration of life. The

Three Graces, Aglaia, Euphrosyne, and Thalia were the daughters of Zeus and Eurynome and their names in Greek mean "radiant", "joyful", and "flo-rescent". They were considered to be the divine protectresses of philoso-phers. From the Hellenis-tic period onwards they were depicted nude and linked one with the other, as laid down by Hesiod. So they appear in Rubens' painting as they generally had been represented, with slight variations, many times since the Renaissance. A subject of such deep Classical roots which has been approached by so many great artists gives rise to many different interpretations, but in Rubens' case it is clear that he painted this work in homage to the divine gifts of beauty, joy, and happiness. Rubens often combined the splendour of the great humanist tradition and his own personal "joie de vivre". Two of the Graces have been identified with the wives of his two happy marriages, Isabella Brandt and Hélène Fourment, the third figure being the ideal summary of the beauty of both. Their faces glow with an almost inexpressive bliss but the quality of the flesh colours of their bodies is astonishing. Their voluptuousness and refinement are reflected in even the smallest detail. Despite the sensuality of these superb nudes, there is not the least hint of piercing desire. Rather, as Kenneth Clark once pointed out, they are haloed with all the cheerful brilliance of a cantata of thanksgiving.

José de Ribera: *Jacob's Dream*
(Cat. No. 1117)

José de Ribera, generally called Jusepe de Ribera in English, was born in Játiva in the region of Valencia in 1591, but he spent most of his life in Italy where he arrived in 1611. His prestige was cemented in Naples, which was under Spanish dominion at that time. Ribera settled in Naples in 1616 and remained there until his death in 1652. He became the lea-

ding figure of the Neapolitan School of the seventeenth century. In spite of his perfect assimilation of Italian art, above all through Caravaggio, Ribera's relationship with his native country never diminished, not only because his principal patrons were the Spanish viceroys but also because the many paintings he sent back to Spain had a very strong impact on the formation of the seventeenth-century Spanish School. One good exam- ple is this *Jacob's Dream*, dated 1639. Together with its companion picture, *The Deliverance of Saint Peter*, it must have been painted for the Duke of Medina de las Torres, who was the viceroy at that time. The two paintings have a symmetrical relationship in their composition, in addition to the common symbolism of sleeping and waking. But the comparatively greater interest of *Jacob's Dream* is due to the fact that the figure of Jacob is presented in a marvellous landscape which has a delicately luminous atmosphere and a subtle sobriety that demonstrates that the nineteenth century was in error in considering Ribera only from the perspective of an impassioned and blood-filled naturalism, because this work is proof of his superb and refined gifts as a colourist. *Jacob's Dream* is the culmination of the change that took place in Ribera's art during the decade of the 1630's when the rather brusque realism of his first period opened up to the influence of the Venetians and the classicism of the Italian Baroque which was prevalent at that moment. Ribera had already painted the patriarchal figure of Jacob on several occasions, but the present work depicts the scene taken from the Book of Genesis in which Jacob was caught by nightfall on his journey from Beersheba to Haran and lay down to sleep in the countryside. There he had a dream in which he saw a ladder that joined Heaven and Earth with angels ascending and descending. In this picture the sky occupies more than half of the composition and in it we find the dazzling luminosity of the ladder that forms a diagonal that seems to surround the recumbent figure of the sleeping Jacob with his legs slightly gathered under. It is a scene that radiates serenity and lyrical peace. The counterpoint of the tree that emerges to the left of the figure of Jacob harmoniously balances the composition which exudes equilibrium in every sense. Neither the intensity and concentration of this painting nor its sober realism manages to destroy its lyricism, emotion, refinement, or even a certain serene idealization.

Diego Velázquez: *Las Meninas, or The Family of Philip IV* (Cat. No. 1174)

This wonderful painting is, without doubt, Velázquez's absolute masterpiece. It was painted in 1656, when the artist was fifty-seven years old, four years before his death. Today the painting is known as Las Meninas, in allusion to the Portuguese term that was used for maids of honour at the Spanish court in the seventeenth century. At that time, the work was referred to at court as the "Picture of the Royal Family". Now it is the principal work of the Prado Museum collection. There are eleven human figures and a mastiff distributed on the frontal and transversal axes of the picture. In the foreground, along an alignment that undulates from left to right according the position of the viewer, we find Velázquez himself, palette and brush in hand, standing at his easel in front of a large canvas that is turned away from us. At his side we see the Infanta Margarita, flanked by two maids of honour in attendance, one of whom is offering the Infanta a drink of water from an earthenware jug. Immediately to the right of the maids of honour and completing the diagonal line, is the dwarf called Maribárbola and next to her, the midget Nicolasito Pertusato, who seems to be trying to rouse the dozing mastiff. In the shadowy middleground we can distinguish the figures of Marcela de Ulloa, *guardadamas menor*, and an unidentified male *guardadamas*. In the background we see the tapestrymaster to the Queen, José Nieto, silhouetted against the light coming through the door that he is either opening or closing. The mirror on the rear wall reflects the image of the King and Queen, whose physical position would coincide with that of the viewer of this pic-

ture. The two groups of figures are distributed throughout the artist's sober and spacious workshop. The depth and height of the room creates a feeling of great emptiness. But the penumbra of this space is cleverly enlivened by the beam of strong light that comes from a window on the right-hand side, to fall directly on the central figure of the Infanta Margarita. Another axis of light crosses the scene from the open door in the background and from the light that bounces off the mirror, reflecting the light of the virtual space where the King and Queen are standing. Velázquez's carefully calculated use of chiaroscuro and his use of both linear and aerial perspective result in the most perfect visual representation ever achieved in the history of painting. Among the many interpretations that have been proposed to explain the motive for this prodigious masterpiece, there are two which are not exclusive of the others: one is of a political and dynastic nature, and the other is the symbolic affirmation of the nobility of painting, emphasized here by the cross of the Order of Santiago painted on Velázquez´s doublet after he was knighted by Philip IV.

Francisco de Zurbarán: *Agnus Dei*
(Cat. No. 7293)

Francisco de Zurbarán was born in 1598 in Fuente de Cantos, in the region of Badajoz in Extremadura, and died in Madrid in 1664, though he lived and worked primarily in Seville. He is considered to be not only one of the greatest masters of the Golden Age but also one of the painters who best represents the sensibility and the characteristics peculiar to the Spanish School. Zurbarán lacked the imagination and cultural background of a Renaissance humanist, but these limitations were compensated for by his deep sense of objective reality and his devotional intensity, which was very much in the spirit of the Counter-Reformation. In this sense, if Zurbarán has often, quite rightly, been cri-

51

ticized for his inexpertness in the correct use of perspective and his awkwardness in grouping his figures in a composition, no one has argued about the profound intensity of his portraits or his astonishing talent for representing even the most humble of objects with chilling realism. His prodigious gift for modelling and his vigorous sense of solid form are displayed in his treatment of drapery and the ornaments of popular costume. So it is not surprising that Zurbarán's genius should be conspicuous in the genre of still-life painting where he is considered to be one of the finest representatives of the distinctively Spanish manner called the *bodegón*. An incomparable example in this area is the beautiful painting known as *Agnus Dei* (Lamb of God), dated 1631. This pious subject lyrically envokes the idea of sacrifice, even though the presence of the animal´s horns or the absence of any religious symbol might indicate that it was a study which the artist made from life with the intention of using it as an element of another composition. Be that as it may, in a subject treated with such humility and sobriety it would be difficult to find greater perfection in the observation of insignificant details such as the lamb´s fleece. Likewise, within the confines of naturalist technique we would be hard put to find deeper emotion in the dramatic treatment of light.

Bartolomé Esteban Murillo: *The Patrician's Dream* (Cat. No. 994)

Murillo was born in Seville towards the end of 1617 and he died in the same city in 1682. He was the first Spanish painter to attain a notable international reputation. Later, and above all during the twentieth century, his reputation unjustifiably declined. This may have been due to the fact that he had become a stereotype who was popular only as a sentimental painter of children and images of the adolescent Virgin Mary. Luckily, in the last twenty years this prejudice has been rectified and at present no one would question the important rôle Murillo played as one of the greatest masters of the Spanish School. He was perhaps the most talented of them all from the standpoint of technical and painterly refinement. This large canvas, originally of semicircular format, was painted around 1662-1665 and its shape tells us that it was originally meant to decorate the Church of Santa María la Blanca in Seville. It is symmetrical to the *Visit to Pope Liberius*, also in the Prado Museum, and the two compositions narrate the story of the founding of the Church of Santa Maria Maggiore in Rome, which took place in the fourth century. The Virgin Mary appeared to the patrician

Johannes and his wife in a dream and told them that they should provide the means for building a church in her honour on the Esquiline Hill, on the spot that would be revealed to them in a snowfall. The first picture relates the dream and the second, the visit the couple made to Pope Liberius to tell him about the dream. The marvellous distribution of light and shade in the *Patrician's Dream* not only directs our attention with the proper dramatic touch, but also leads us skillfully into the deep shadows of the chamber and emphasizes the features of the principal figures and the everyday objects with exquisite lyricism. A restrained silence pervades the whole scene in which everything seems to merge harmoniously in the midst of a beatific calm. The very subtle orchestration of the whole composition also reveals Murillo's prodigious virtuosity in handling even the most insignificant details with surprising expressiveness.

Francisco de Goya: *The Family of Charles IV*
(Cat. No. 726)

This work was painted in 1800, when Goya was fifty-four years old and at the height of his artistic career and his life at Court, even though he was already suffering from the aftereffects of the serious illness that had left him completely deaf in the previous decade. *The Family of Charles IV* is not only one of Goya's masterpieces, it is also one of the finest works in the history of portraiture. Goya's talent for portraiture was prodigious in its psychological insight and modernity. This is a group portrait of the Royal Family and because of the nature of the subject matter, comparisons are often made with Las Meninas by Velázquez, a painter whom Goya always admired, and *The Family of Philip V* by the French painter, Louis-Michel van Loo. Like Velázquez, Goya has included himself alongside the eminent company, although somewhat more discreetly. Formally speaking, the three great group portraits have very little in common, but their traditional emplacement in the Prado Museum forms visual diagonals that visitors never fail to notice. The fourteen figures that appear in Goya's picture are distributed along a sinuous alignment the centre of which is occupied by the powerful, plump figure of Queen María Luisa who holds her younger son, the Infante Francisco de Paula, by the hand in a protective gesture as she places her other arm around the shoulders of her younger daughter, the Infanta María Isabel. The figure of Charles IV is slightly dislocated and appears less splendid because of the dark colour of his costume, just as the light blue coat of the heir to the throne, Fernando, Prince of Asturias, who is standing on the left, loses

some of its brilliance because the figure is partly bathed in shadows. From a dramatic point of view, these two figures seem less important, even though both of them are standing somewhat more forward than the Queen herself. Pressed behind them, in a discreet middle distance, is the rest of the family, in this order: behind the Prince of Asturias is the king's second son, the Infante Carlos Isidro María; the king's sister, the Infanta María Josefa; and a young woman whose face is turned away and whose identity is still under debate. Further towards the background, in an almost total penumbra, we see Goya working on this portrait. Behind the King we see the heads of the his brother, the Infante Antonio Pascual; the Infanta Carlota Joaquina, who had already become queen of Portugal; and the full-length figures of the Princes of Parma, Luis and María Luisa Josefina who is holding her son, the Infante Carlos Luis, in her arms. The extraordinary sense of naturalism with which Goya imbues this scene and the stark candour with which he depicts each one of the personages have given rise to interpretations which maintain that the painter wanted to caricature his illustrious sitters, or even stigmatize the image of a dying monarchy. Such ideas are as suggestive as they are improbable.

OTHER RECOMMENDED MASTERPIECES

LOWER FLOOR

1. **Antonello da Messina:** The Dead Christ Sustained by an Angel. No. 3092. Room 49.
2. **Bermejo:** Saint Dominic of Silos Enthroned as Abbot. No. 1323. Room 57b.
3. **Memling:** The Adoration of the Magi. No. 1557. Room 58a.
4. **Bosch:** The Tabletop of the Seven Deadly Sins. No. 2822. Room 56a.
5. **Dürer:** Self-Portrait. No. 2179. Room 54.
6. **Moro:** Mary Tudor. No. 2108. Room 55b.
7. **Correggio:** The Virgin Mary, the Christ Child, and St. John. No. 112. Room 49.
8. **Titian:** Danaë. No. 425. Room 61b.
9. **Titian:** Bacchanal. No. 418. Room 61b.
10. **Titian:** Philip II. No. 411. Room 61.
11. **El Greco:** The Holy Trinity. No. 824. Sala 62a.
12. **Sánchez Coello:** Infanta Isabella Clara Eugenia. No. 1137. Room 63a.

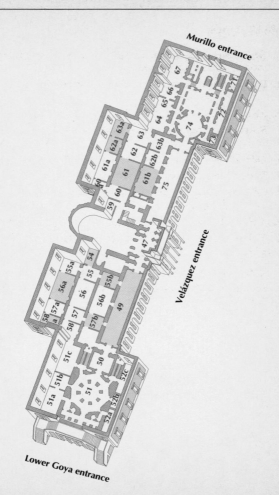

Murillo entrance

Velázquez entrance

Lower Goya entrance

OTHER RECOMMENDED MASTERPIECES

FIRST FLOOR

13. **"Velvet" Brueghel:** The Five Senses. Nos. 1394, 1395, 1396, 1397, 1398. Room 8.

14. **Rubens:** The Garden of Love. No. 1690. Room 9.

15. **Rubens:** The Adoration of the Magi. No. 1638. Room 9b.

16. **Ribera:** The Deliverance of St. Peter. No. 1073. Room 26.

17. **Velázquez:** Vulcan's Forge. No. 1171. Room 12.

18. **Velázquez:** Christ Crucified. No. 1167. Room 15.

19. **Velázquez:** The Surrender of Breda. No. 1172. Room 16.

20. **Murillo:** The "El Escorial" Immaculate Conception. No 972. Room 28.

21. **Goya:** "Black Paintings": The Dog. No. 767. Room 36.

22. **Goya:** "Black Paintings": Duel with Cudgels. No. 758. Room 37.

23. **Goya:** "Black Paintings": Witches' Sabbath. No. 761. Room 38.

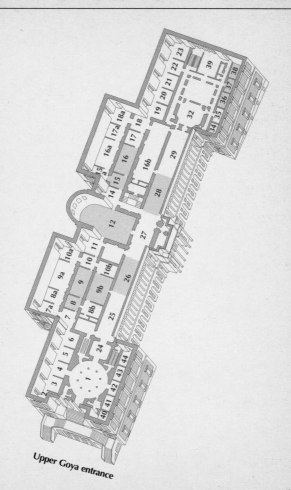

Upper Goya entrance

Bibliography

ALVAREZ LOPERA, J., El Greco la obra esencial. Madrid, 1993.

ANGULO IÑIGUEZ, D., Museo del Prado. Pintura italiana anterior a 1660. Madrid, 1979.

ANZELEWSKY, F., DÜRER, His Art and Life. Freiburg, 1980.

BALIS, A., etc., La pintura flamenca en el Museo del Prado. Antwerp, 1989.

BANGO, I., MARÍAS, F., Bosch. Realidad, símbolo y fantasía. Vitoria, 1982.

BEROQUI, P., Tiziano en el Museo del Prado, Madrid, 1946.

BROWN, J. Y ELLIOTT, J.H., A Palace for a King: The Buen Retiro and the Court of Philip IV. New Haven - New York, 1980.

BROWN, J.. Imágenes e ideas en la pintura española del XVII. Madrid, 1985.

CALVO SERRALLER, F., Las Meninas de Velázquez. Madrid, 1995.

Exhibition catalogue, Rafael en España. Museo del Prado, 1985.

Exhibition catalogue, Zurbarán. Museo del Prado. Madrid, 1988.

Exhibition catalogue, Velázquez. Museo del Prado, Madrid, 1990.

Exhibition catalogue, Rembrandt. Le Maître et son atelier, Paris, 1991.

Exhibition catalogue, Ribera 1591-1652. Museo del Prado, Madrid 1992.

Exhibition catalogue, De Tiziano a Bassano. Maestros venecianos del Museo del Prado. M.N.A.C., Barcelona, 1997

Exhibition catalogue, El jardín de las delicias de El Bosco: copias, estudio técnico y restauración, Museo del Prado, Madrid, 2000.

CHECA, F., Tiziano y la Monarquía Hispánica. Madrid, 1994.

CHERRY, P., Arte y naturaleza. El bodegón español en el Siglo de Oro. Madrid, 1999.

DAVIES, M., Rogier van der Weyden, and essay, with critical catalogue of paintings assigned, Londres, 1972.

DÍAZ PADRÓN, M., Museo del Prado. El siglo de Rubens en el Museo del Prado: catálogo razonado de la pintura flamenca del S. XVII, 3 volúmenes, Barcelona, 1996.

FALKENBURG, R.L., Joachim Patenier. Landscape as an Image of the Pilgrimage of Life. Amsterdam – Philadelphia, 1988.

FALOMIR, M., Pintura italiana del Renacimiento. Museo del Prado. Madrid, 1999.

FREEDBERG, S, J., Pintura en Italia 1500/1600. Madrid, 1978.

GÁLLEGO, J., Visión y símbolos en la pintura española del Siglo de Oro. Madrid, 1992.

GARRRIDO, C., Velázquez, técnica y evolución. Madrid, 1992.

GASSIER, P., WILSON, J.: Goya. His Life and Work. London, 1971.

GIBSON, W.S., Hieronymus Bosch. London, 1973.

MARÍAS, F., El Greco, biografía de un pintor extravagante. Madrid, 1997.

MARÍAS, F., Las Meninas. Madrid, 1999.

OBERHUBER, K., Raphael. The Paintings. Munich, London, New York, 1999.

PALLUCHINI, P., Veronese. Barcelona, 1984.

PALLUCHINI, P, Y ROSSI, P.: Tintoretto. Le opere sacre e profane. Milan,1990.

PANOFSKY. E., Vida y arte de Alberto Durero, Madrid, 1982.

PÉREZ SÁNCHEZ, A. E., Pintura barroca española 1600-1750, Madrid, 1992.

PHILIPPOT, P., La peinture dans les anciens Pays-Bas, XV-XVIe siécles, Paris, 1994.

PIGNATTI, T., Veronese, Milán, 1976.

RUÍZ MANERO, J.M., Pintura italiana del siglo XVI en España. Tomo II. Rafael y su escuela, Madrid, 1996.

SANTOS, PADRE FRANCISCO DE LOS, Descripción breve del Monasterio de S. Lorenzo el Real del Escorial única maravilla del mundo..., Madrid, 1657, 1667,1681 y 1698.

SIGÜENZA, FRAY JOSÉ DE, Tercera parte de la Historia de la Orden de San Jerónimo, Doctor de la Iglesia, Madrid, 1600-1605.

THUILLIER, J., Obra pictórica completa de Poussin, Barcelona, 1973.

Various authors, El Siglo de Oro de la pintura española, Madrid, 1991.

Various authors, El retrato en el Museo del Prado Madrid, 1994.

Various authors, El Museo del Prado. Amberes, 1996.

Various authors, Obras maestras del Museo del Prado, Madrid, 1996.

Various authors, El desnudo en el Museo del Prado, Barcelona, 1998.

Various authors, Velázquez, Barcelona. 1999.

Various authors, Goya. Barcelona, 2002.

Various authors, Historias inmortales, Barcelona, 2002.

Various authors, Goya. La familia de Carlos IV. Madrid, 2002.

YARZA LUACES, J., El jardín de las delicias de El Bosco. Madrid, 1998.

General Information on the Prado Museum

EDIFICIO VILLANUEVA
Paseo del Prado, s/n
28014 Madrid
Telephone: 91 330.28.00
Fax: 91 330.28.56
Wheelchair access available

MUSEUM OPENING HOURS
*Tuesday to Sunday and
public holidays:*
9:00 a.m. to 7:00 p.m.
(Last entry 30 minutes before
closing. Visitors are requested
to start vacating the galleries
10 minutes before closing.)
*Closed on Mondays
1 January, Good Friday,
1 May and 25 December*

ADMISSION CHARGES
Basic Admission: 3 €
*Discounted admission
(with ID):*   1,5 €
• Holders of youth cards, students'
cards or international equivalents.
• Cultural and educational groups
(by prior arrangement).
• Members of national or interna-
tional museum associations.

Free admission (with ID):
• Visitors under 18.
• Visitors over 65, pensioners,
registered disabled.
• Unemployed.
• Members of the *Fundación Ami-
gos del Museo del Prado.*
• Cultural and educational volun-
teers (by prior arrangement).
Free admission for all:
Sundays from 9 a.m. to 7:00 p.m.
18 May (International Museums
Day).

12 October (National Holiday).
6 December (Constitution Day).

Cafeteria
Tuesday to Sunday and public
holidays from 9 a.m. to 6:20 p.m.
24 and 31 December from 9 a.m.
to 1:20 p.m.

Restaurant
Tuesday to Sunday and public
holidays from 11:30 a.m. to 4 p.m.

Shops
Tuesday to Sunday and public
holidays from 9 a.m. to 6:30 p.m.
24 and 31 December from
9 a.m. to 1:30 p.m.

HOW TO GET THERE
Metro: Atocha, Banco and Retiro
stations.
Bus: Numbers 9, 10, 14, 19, 27,
34, 37, 45
From the airport:
Airport shuttle bus to Plaza de
Colón, then bus No. 27.

General Information about the Fundación Amigos del Museo del Prado
Museo del Prado
c/ Ruiz de Alarcón, nº 21 – bajo.
28014 Madrid
Tel: 91 420.20.46
Fax.: 91 429.50.20
E-mail: famprado@canaldata.es
web: www.amigosmuseoprado.org

Office hours:
Monday to Friday, from 9:30 a.m.
to 2:30 p.m.